Phonics Playlets
SHORT VOWELS

20 Reproducible Decodable Plays That Boost Key Reading & Fluency Skills

LIZA CHARLESWORTH

SCHOLASTIC

Publisher: Tara Welty
Editor: Ourania Papacharalambous
Cover design: Cynthia Ng
Cover illustrations: Rob McClurkan
Interior design: Jaime Lucero
Interior illustrations: Rob McClurkan

ISBN 978-1-5461-5532-4

Scholastic Inc., 557 Broadway, New York, NY 10012

First printing, February 2025

1 2 3 4 5 6 7 8 9 10 40 34 33 32 31 30 29 28 27 26 25

Contents

NOTE: To locate a playlet, refer to the page numbers that appear sideways on the scripts.
The numbers in gray circles (located at the bottom of the pages) show the sequence of each playlet.

Introduction

Research shows that nearly 84 percent of words in the English language are decodable. That means children with a strong grasp of phonics are on course to develop into effective readers. But how do you reinforce key phonemic elements to help every child become confident, agile, and fluent?

The answer is *Phonics Playlets: Short Vowels*! This dramatically fun resource provides the practice required to master essential phonics concepts and build important oral-language skills. The 20 playlets in this book are highly decodable and highly engaging, with funny plots to motivate children to learn alongside their classmates!

In addition, *Phonics Playlets: Short Vowels* includes these literacy-boosting features:

- A variety of playlets, each focusing on a different must-know phonics concept (such as short *a*) or reviewing those concepts
- Big, easy-to-read type paired with playful illustrations
- Highly decodable text based on a knowledge of essential high-frequency words (*be, my, the, see, what*) and the ability to sound out regular consonant-vowel-consonant words (*cat, pen, pig, dog, bug*) plus simple words that are plural or end in double letters or *-ck* (*jazz, mess, peck, duck*)

What else makes this an optimal learning resource? The collection includes playlets for two to five readers, which makes them perfect for partner practice as well as small-group lessons. You can even send them home, enabling children to build must-know phonics skills with their loved ones!

On the pages that follow, you'll find quick tips to make using these playlets an effective—and joyful—component of your literacy program. So, get started today and "set the stage" for your students to become fluent readers and confident speakers.

Happy learning!

P.S. Be sure to graduate to the companion sets, *Phonics Playlets: Long Vowels* and *Phonics Playlets: Blends & Digraphs.*

7 Quick Tips for Using the Playlets

The playlets in this book were designed for flexible use, but here are some tips to maximize learning.

1. **Preview each playlet before assigning it to children.** Check the number of readers, length, and text as well as the high-frequency and stretch-word lists to ensure the playlet is a good match for learners. (*Stretch words* are words that are tricky and/or nondecodable.) Note that each of the first five playlets focuses on a specific vowel sound (such as short *a*), so they are just right for children at the beginning of their literacy journey.

2. **Select a playlet to use with partners or a small group.** For example, you can choose to pair a striving reader with a strong "mentor" reader or group children at the same basic reading level. **TIP:** You might consider including an adult aide in the mix to provide real-time help with decoding.

3. **Select roles for children or allow them to choose.** Many of the roles have roughly the same number of lines, which makes this an easy process. Prior to embarking on a playlet, encourage children to activate their imaginations and be open to playing a wide variety of characters.

4. **Reproduce the playlet, providing each reader with a copy.** Before reading, have children review the high-frequency words and stretch words listed at the top right corner of the script. A familiarity with these words will help facilitate fluency. **TIP:** Consider using highlighter pens to assist individuals in locating their lines.

Fun & Effective Ways to Use the Playlets

- Boost phonics knowledge—and fun!—by giving children a few minutes to locate and underline all the words in a playlet that relate to its focus skill; for example, words with short *a* (*cat, bat, nap,* etc.) in *Cat and Bat.*
- Challenge pairs or small groups to practice the playlets and perform them for the rest of the class.
- Encourage children to record audio versions of the playlets, placing them in your listening center for classmates to access and enjoy.
- Provide craft materials, such as ice cream sticks or paper bags, so children can create puppet characters to enhance their readings of the playlets.
- Send the playlets home for children to read along with family members.

5. **Encourage learners to help one another sound out decodable words and read high-frequency words.** In addition, challenge children to be mindful of punctuation and attempt to read their lines with the proper inflection for sentences that end in periods, exclamation points, and question marks.

6. **Boost comprehension by following up a playlet with a meaningful text-dependent question.** Upon reading *The Hot Dog*, for example, you might ask: *What was the dog's problem? How did he solve that problem?* Children can respond orally or in writing.

7. **Invite children to read a playlet several times to polish their reading and oral-language skills.** On second and third readings, learners can work to improve their pacing, pronunciation, and inflection. Research shows that rereading promotes confidence and fluency. There is no such thing as enjoying a text too many times.

Connection to the Standards

The lessons in this book support the College and Career Readiness Anchor Standards for Reading. These broad standards, which serve as the basis of many state standards, were developed to establish rigorous educational expectations with the goal of providing students nationwide with a quality education that prepares them for college and careers. The chart below details how the lessons and activities align with specific reading standards for students in Grades K–3.

Foundational Skills

Print Concepts

- Demonstrate understanding of the organization and basic features of print.
- Follow words from left to right, top to bottom, and page by page.
- Recognize that spoken words are represented in written language by specific sequences of letters.
- Understand that words are separated by spaces in print.
- Recognize and name all uppercase and lowercase letters of the alphabet.
- Recognize the distinguishing features of a sentence (e.g., first word, capitalization, ending punctuation).

Phonics and Word Recognition

- Know and apply grade-level phonics and word analysis skills in decoding words.
- Demonstrate basic knowledge of one-to-one letter-sound correspondences.
- Associate the short and long sounds with the common spellings for the five major vowels.
- Distinguish between similarly spelled words by identifying the sounds of the letters that differ.
- Decode regularly spelled one-syllable words.
- Use knowledge that every syllable must have a vowel sound to determine the number of syllables in a printed word.
- Recognize and read grade-appropriate irregularly spelled words.

Fluency

- Read emergent-reader texts with purpose and understanding.
- Read grade-level text orally with accuracy, appropriate rate, and expression on successive readings.
- Use context to confirm or self-correct word recognition and understanding, rereading as necessary.
- Actively engage in group reading activities with purpose and understanding.

Cat and Bat

2 Characters

High-Frequency Words
be, we,
and, the

Stretch Word
band

Cat: I am a cat.

Bat: I am a bat.

Cat: Can a cat and a bat
be pals?

Bat: Yes, we can!

Cat: A cat and a bat can gab.

Cat + Bat: Gab, gab, gab.

Bat: A cat and a bat can nap.

Cat: Zzzzzzzzzzz.

Bat: Can a cat and a bat be in a band?

Cat: Yes, we can!

Bat: I can rap and tap.

Cat: I can jam on a sax.

Bat: Rap, tap, rap, tap!

Cat: Jam, jam, jam!

Bat: Not bad!

Cat: The Cat and Bat Band is fab!

Bat: Cats can be fans.

Cat: Bats can be fans.

Cat + Bat: Rap, tap, jam, jam!

Mel's Pet Hen

2 Characters

Mel	Jen

High-Frequency Words
do, no, my, and, the, you, what

Stretch Word
best

Mel: I am Mel.

Jen: I am Jen.

Mel: Jen is my pet red hen!

Jen: Yes, I am.

Mel: Jen, let's get on a jet.

Jen: No, Mel. I can not.

Mel: Jen, let's get gum. Yum!

Jen: No, Mel. I can not.

Mel: What CAN you do, Jen?

Jen: Well, I can get in my pen.

Mel: I bet you can, Jen.

Jen: I can peck, peck, peck.

Mel: I bet you can, Jen.

Jen: I can sit on my eggs.

Mel: I bet you can, Jen.

Jen: My eggs can pop, pop, pop!

Mel: What is in the eggs, Jen?

Jen: Bev and Ken and Jem!

Mel: Bev, Ken, and Jem are the best!

Jen: Yes, yes, yes!

Up the Big Hill

2 Characters

High-Frequency Words
be, we, do,
of, to, the,
down, what

Stretch Word
roll

Kit: I am Kit. I am six.

Pig: I am Kit's pet pig.

Kit: Let's zip up the big hill.

Pig: OK, it is fun to zip up a hill.

Kit + Pig: Run, run, run. Up, up, up.

Kit: We did it! We got to the top of the hill.

Pig: The top is fun. But what can we do?

Kit: We can kick a tin can.

Pig: We can dig a pit.

Kit: We can sit in the sun.

Pig: Yes, let's sit in the sun.

Kit + Pig: Sit, sit, sit. Sun, sun, sun.

Kit: The sun will set in a bit.

Pig: Yes, let's zip down the big hill.

Kit: OK. Run, run, run. I fell!

Pig: Run, run, run. I fell as well!

Kit: Do not be sad, Pig. We can roll.

Pig: OK, Kit. It will be fun to roll.

Kit + Pig: Roll, roll, roll. Fun, fun, fun.

Pig: It is fun to zip up a hill.

Kit: It fun to roll down a hill as well!

The Hot Dog

2 Characters

High-Frequency Words
be, we, of, so, to, and, the

Stretch Word
pond

Dog: I am a dog. I can run.

Fox: I am a fox. I can run as well.

Dog: Let's jog to the log, Fox.

Dog + Fox: Jog, jog to the log!

Fox: Yes! We got to the log.

Dog: But the log is in the sun,
so I am a hot dog.

Fox: It is NOT fun to be hot.
Let's jog to the rock.

Dog + Fox: Jog, jog to the rock!

Fox: Yes! We got to the rock.

Dog: But the rock is in the sun,
so I am a hot dog.

Fox: It is NOT fun to be hot.
Let's jog to the pond.

Dog + Fox: Jog, jog to the pond!

Fox: Yes! We got to the pond.

Dog: But the pond is in the sun,
so I am a hot dog.

Fox: It is NOT fun to be hot.
But I can fix it, Dog.
Let's hop in the pond.

Dog + Fox: Hop, hop in the pond!

Fox: The pond is wet and lots of fun.

Dog: Yes! I am NOT a hot dog.

Pug and Cub

2 Characters

High-Frequency Words
we, of, my, and, are, see, the

Stretch Words
dump, jump

Pug: I am a pug. My pal is a cub!

Cub: I am a cub. My pal is a pug!

Pug: Let's run and jump in the mud.

Cub: OK. Run, run, run.

Pug: Huff, puff, huff, puff.

Cub: We are at the mud.

Pug: 1, 2, 3. Jump in!

Cub: Mud is fun, but mud is a mess.

Pug: Yup. Yuck, yuck, yuck!

Cub: Let's run and jump in the tub.

Pug: OK. Run, run, run.

Cub: Huff, puff, huff, puff.

Pug: We are at the tub.

Cub: 1, 2, 3. Jump in!

Pug: We are in the tub.

Cub: Yup. See the jug? It has suds.

Pug: Let's dump in the suds.

Cub: OK. Suds, suds, suds.

Pug: A pug and a cub in a tub of suds is a lot of fun.

Cub: Yup. Fun, fun, fun!

Ned Has a Nap

2 Characters

High-Frequency Words
no, or, to, my, and, are, why, you, your, have, want

Stretch Words
spot, snug

Sal: I am Sal. I am a kid.

Ned: I am Ned. I am a big bug.

Sal: Ned is my pet. Ned is fab!

Ned: I am fab, but sad. Sob, sob!

Sal: Why are you sad, Ned?

Ned: Sob, sob! I want to nap.
But I do not have a spot.

Sal: I will let you nap in my hat.

Ned: No! Your hat is snug, but it is hot.

Sal: I will let you nap in my tub.

Ned: No! Your tub is snug, but it is wet.

Sal: I will let you nap on my mat.

Ned: No! Your mat is snug,
but it has gum on it. YUCK!

Sal: I will let you nap in my mug.

Ned: Yes! Your mug is snug.
It is not hot or wet.
It has no gum on it.

Sal: And my mug has a bed in it.
Hop in, Ned!

Ned: OK. Hop, hop. Zzzzzzzzzzzz!

Sal: Ned is as snug as a bug in my mug.

Gus Has Gum!

2 Characters

High-Frequency Words
be, me, hi, of, my, see, the, you, have, like, make, what, with, little

Stretch Word
bubble

Gus: Hi Viv! I got it! I got it!

Viv: Hi Gus! What did you get?

Gus: I got a big bag of gum.

Viv: But gum can be bad.
It can make a mess.

Gus: No, Viv. Gum is NOT bad.
I like gum! I like gum!

Viv: OK, Gus. Have fun with the gum!

Gus: Yum, yum! See my bubble?

Viv: Yes, Gus. I can see it is little.

Gus: Yum, yum! See my bubble?

Viv: Yes, Gus. I can see it is big.

Gus: Yum, yum, yum, yum! POP!

Viv: Yuck, Gus! I can see a mess.
A lot of gum is on you!

Gus: Can you get me a wet rag, Viv?

Viv: OK, Gus. You can rub off
the gum with the rag.

Gus: Yes. Rub, rub. No gum.

Viv: Gus, you did a fab job!
You got rid of the mess.

Gus: Yes, Viv. Can you get my bag?
I like gum! I like gum!

Viv: Gus, did you miss it?
If a gum bubble pops,
it will make a mess.

Gus: Yes, Viv. But you got me a wet rag so I can get rid of the mess.

Viv: OK, Gus. Have fun with the gum!

Gus: I will. Yum, yum, yum!

Sad, Mad Pals

2 Characters

High-Frequency Words
be, do, no, to, my, and, the, you, have, like, then

Stretch Words
best, sorry

Cat: I am a cat. I have dots.

Pup: I am pup. I am tan.

Cat: Pup is my best bud!

Pup: Cat is my best bud!

Cat: Pup, let's run and sit in the box.

Pup: No! A box is not fun.
Let's jog in the sun.

Cat: No! A jog will be hot.
Let's dig in the mud.

Pup: No! Mud is a mess.
Let's nap on the rug.

Cat: I do not like to nap.
I am mad at you, Pup!

Pup: Well, I am mad at you, Cat!
Mad, mad, mad!

Cat: Then I will run off
and sit in the box.

Pup: Then I will run off
and nap on the rug.

Cat: Huff, puff! I ran to the box.

Pup: Huff, puff! I ran to the rug.

Cat: The box is not a bit fun.
I miss my best bud, Pup.

Pup: The rug in not a bit fun.
I miss my best bud, Cat.

Cat: It is bad to be sad.
I will run and get Pup.

Pup: It is bad to be mad.
I will run and get Cat.

Cat + Pup: Huff, puff! Run, run!

Cat: Sob, sob! I am sorry, Pup.

Pup: Sob, sob! I am sorry, Cat.

Cat: I do not like to be sad.

Pup: I do not like to be mad.

Cat: But I DO like to be best buds.

Pup: Yes, best bud! Let's hug.

Cat + Pup: Hug, hug!

Liz Can Get a Pet

2 Characters

High-Frequency Words
be, do, no, and, see, the

Stretch Word
forest

Liz: Mom, I am ten. Can I get a pet?

Mom: Yes, Liz. You can!

Liz: Let's go on a jog in the forest.

Mom: Yes, let's. I bet you will see a pet to get.

Liz + Mom: Jog, jog, jog, jog!

Liz: I see a red fox! Can it be a pet?

Mom: No, Liz. A fox is not a kid's pet.

Liz + Mom: Jog, jog, jog, jog!

Liz: I see a big bat. Can it be a pet?

Mom: No, Liz. A bat is not a kid's pet.

Liz: I see a tan bug. Can it be a pet?

Mom: No, Liz. A bug is not a kid's pet.

Liz: I do not see a pet yet.
I am sad, Mom.

Mom: Do not be sad, Liz. I bet
you will see a pet in a bit.

Liz + Mom: Jog, jog, jog, jog!

Liz: I see a rock. Can it be a pet?

Mom: Yes, Liz. A rock CAN be a kid's pet.

Liz: I will pick up the rock and pat it.
Pat, pat, pat, pat.

Mom: A rock will not yip or yap.
It can sit on a mat.
It can nap on a bed.

Liz: Pat, pat, pat, pat.
A rock is a fun pet, Mom!

Mom: Yes, Liz. It is!

Log Hop

2 Characters

High-Frequency Words
we, do, to, my, and, are, our, see, the, why, you, have, with, happy

Stretch Word
frog

Max: I am Max. I am a frog.

Deb: I am Deb. I am a frog as well.

Max: I see a big log. Let's hop on it.

Deb: OK, Max. Let's!

Max + Deb: Hop, hop on the log!

Deb: It is fun to hop on the log.

Max: Yes, but I am a bit sad, Deb.

Deb: Why are you sad, Max?

Max: I am sad I do not have my hat on.

Deb: Yes, I miss my hat as well.

Max: Let's get our hats and hop on the log.

Deb: OK, Max. Let's!

Max + Deb: Hop, hop on the log in our hats!

Deb: It is fun to hop on the log in our hats.

Max: Yes, but I am a bit sad, Deb.

Deb: Why are you sad, Max?

Max: I am sad I do not have my socks on.

Deb: Yes, I miss my socks as well.

Max: Let's get our socks and hop on the log.

Deb: OK, Max. Let's!

Max + Deb: Hop, hop on the log
in our hats and socks!

Max: Deb, I am happy, happy, happy!

Deb: Why are you happy, Max?

Max: I get to hop on the log in a hat and socks with my frog pal, Deb.

Deb: Yes, we can hop 'til the sun sets!

Max: Hop, hop on the log...

Deb: in our hats and socks!

Tam's Web

2 Characters

High-Frequency Words
be, we, hi, of, do, to, my, you, down, have, help, what, when, with, your

Stretch Words
home, stuck

Tam: Hi! I am Tam.

Bud: Hi! I am Bud.

Tam: I am red with 8 legs.

Bud: I am tan with 8 legs.

Tam: My home is a web.

Bud: My home is a rock.

Tam: Can we be pals?

Bud: I bet we can, Tam!

Tam: Fab! Will you hop up to my web, Bud?

Bud: Yes! But I have to hop back down to my rock at ten.

Tam: OK. I will tell you when it is ten.

Bud: Hop, hop, hop. BIG hop!

Tam: You did it! You got up to my web.

Bud: Yes! But what can we do in it?

Tam: We can sit for a bit.

Tam + Bud: Sit, sit, sit, sit, sit.

Tam: We can nap for a bit.

Tam + Bud: Nap, nap, nap, nap, nap. Zzzzzzzzzzzzzzzzzz!

Tam: Get up, Bud! It is ten.

Bud: Hop, hop, hop. Yuck! I am stuck in your web.

Tam: I can help. You hop as I tug.

Bud: OK. Hop, hop, hop. BIG hop!

Tam: Tug, tug, tug. BIG tug!

Bud: POP! I am NOT stuck in your web.

Tam: Yes! But I will miss you a lot, Bud.
I am sad. Sob, sob, sob!

Bud: Do not be sad and sob, Tam.
If you hop down to my rock,
you will not miss me a bit.

Tam: OK. I bet your rock will be a lot of fun.

Bud: Yes! And I bet you will NOT get stuck.

Kim Is Six!

2 Characters

High-Frequency Words
be, we, my, to, and, for, say, the, you, play, make, what, wish, happy

Stretch Words
birthday, thanks, cake

Kim: I am six! I am six!

Tod: Happy birthday, Kim!
I got a hat for you.

Kim: Thanks, Tod! I will pop it on.
Can we play tag?

Tod: OK. You can be it.

Kim + Tod: Run, run, run, run.

Kim: Tag, Tod! I got you.

Tod: Yes, Kim! You did. You won tag.

Kim: It is fun to win on my birthday!

Tod: Kim, I got a big cake for you!
You can make a wish.

Kim: Thanks, Tod! I did make a wish.

Tod: What did you wish for, Kim?

Kim: I can not tell you, Tod.

Tod: Kim, I got a big box for you.

Kim: Thanks, Tod. But the box will not sit.
It says "Ruff!" and runs off.

Tod: Yes, Kim! The box is odd. Pop the top off and see what is in it.

Kim: OK, Tod. I will. POP!
A pug is in the box!

Tod: The pug can run and play.
It can say "Ruff!"

Kim: Yes! I am a happy gal.
The pug can be my pet.
Thanks, Tod. I got my wish!

Pen, Pad, and Rat

3 Characters

High-Frequency Words
be, me, we, hi, do, my, to, all, and, you, have, what, wish, with

Stretch Word
draw

Pen: Hi! I am a red pen.

Pad: Hi! I am a big pad.

Rat: Hi! I am a pet rat.

Pen: I wish I had a pal!

Pad: I wish I had a pal!

Rat: I wish I had a pal!

Pen: Well, I can be pals with a big pad.

Pad: Well, I can be pals with a red pen.

Rat: Well, I can be pals with a big pad
AND a red pen.

All: Yes, yes, yes! We can all be pals.

Pen: OK. But what can we do to have fun?

Rat: Well, Pen, you can draw on Pad.

Pad: Yes, Pen. You can draw on me in red.

Pen: OK, Pad. But what can I draw?

Pad: I got it! Pen, you can draw Rat.

Rat: Yes! You can draw me in my cap.
I can run to my hut and get it.

Pen: Yes! Run and get the cap, Rat.

Rat: Zip, zap! I am back
and I have my cap on.
I am all set!

Pad: I am all set as well, Rat.
Sit on the rock in the sun
and Pen will draw you in red.

Pen: Draw, draw, draw, draw.
It is fun to draw Rat on Pad.

Pad: Yes! Rat in his cap is fab!

Rat: What luck to be pals with Pad and Pen!

Tess Is a Mess!

3 Characters

High-Frequency Words
be, we, hi, my, of, her, and, the, then, little

Stretch Words
best, talk

Ross: Hi, I am Ross. Jazz is my big sis.

Jazz: Hi, I am Jazz. Tess is my little sis.

Ross: Can you say "Hi," Tess?

Tess: Bap, bap, bap.

Jazz: Tess is the best little sis.

Ross: Yup! But Tess can not talk yet.

Jazz: And Tess is a mess!

Tess: Dub, dub, dub.

Ross: Yup! Tess got jam on her lips.

Jazz: Then, Tess got yams on her top.

Tess: Nem, nem, nem.

Ross: Then Tess got big gobs of mud on her little cap.

Tess: Lop, lop, lop.

Jazz: Yup! Tess is a BIG, BIG, BIG mess!

Ross: YUCK!

Jazz: But we can fix it.

Ross: Yup! Let's get Tess in the tub.

Tess: Bup, bup, bup.

Jazz: Let's get Tess her little duck.

Tess: Mib, mib, mib.

Ross: In the tub, Tess will get rid of the jam, yams, and mud.

Tess: Wab, wab, wab.

Jazz: Then Tess can get a bib.

Ross: Yup! The bib will let Tess be less of a mess!

Tess: Din, din, din.

Jazz: Tess can not talk yet…

Ross: But Tess is the best little sis!

Tess: Gad, gad, gad.

The Bugs and the Ram

3 Characters

High-Frequency Words
be, we, hi, do, go, of, to, and, our, the, you, have, want, what, little

Stretch Words
fast, ice cream

Bess: Hi, I am Bess! I am a little bug.

Beck: Hi, I am Beck!
I am a little bug as well.

Bess: Let's go and see our pal, Ron.

Beck: OK. Ron is a lot of fun.

Bess + Beck: Zig, zag, bizz, buzz to Ron.

Ron: Hi, little bugs. I am a ram.
I am big! I can run fast!

Bess: I am sad. I want to be as big as Ron.

Beck: I am sad. I want to run as fast as Ron.

Bess + Beck: Sob, sob, sob, sob!

Ron: Do not sob, little bugs.
You are not big.
You can not run fast.
But you can do a lot.

Bess: What can 2 little bugs do?

Beck: Yes! Tell us, Ron.

Ron: Well, you can zig and zag.

Bess: Yes, Ron. We can!

Ron: And you can bizz and buzz.

Beck: Yes, Ron. We can!

Ron: Let's have fun. I will run.
You will zig, zag and bizz, buzz.

Bess: OK. 1, 2, 3…

Beck: Get set, go!

Ron: Run, run, run, run.

Bess + Beck: Zig, zag, bizz, buzz.

Ron: Run, run, run, run.

Bess + Beck: Zig, zag, bizz, buzz.

Ron: You see! Big and little pals can have a lot of fun.

Bess: Yes, Ron. We can!

Beck: Big and little pals can go to the Ice Cream Hut as well.

Bess: Yes, Ron. We can!

Ron: I will run to the hut.

Beck: Bess and I will zig, zag and bizz, buzz to the hut.

Ron: OK. Run, run, run, run.

Bess + Beck: Zig, zag, bizz, buzz.

Ron: Run, run, run, run.

Bess + Beck: Zig, zag, bizz, buzz.

Ron: We got to the hut, Bess and Beck.

Bess: Yes, Ron. We did it!

Beck: We can get ice cream.

Bess + Beck: OK. Let's!

All: Yum, yum, yum!

Will Zak Say "Yum"?

3 Characters

High-Frequency Words
be, me, we, do, of, to, my, and, are, say, you, have, like, with

Stretch Word
food

Min: I am Min. I am ten.

Zak: I am Zak. I am six.

Dad: I am Dad. Min and Zak are my kids.

Min: I like lots of food. I say "Yum" a lot.

Zak: I do NOT like lots of food.
I fuss and say "Yuck" a lot.

Dad: Min, let's fix Zak a hot cup
of mud to sip.

Min: Yes, Dad. I bet we can get
him to say "Yum."

Zak: I will not say "Yum," but I will say "Yuck."

Dad: Min, get me a big pot.

Min: OK, Dad. I got a big pot.

Dad: I will fill it up with mud.
Mud, mud, mud!

Min: I will mix in jam.
Jam, jam, jam!

Dad: I will mix in gum.
Gum, gum, gum!

Min: I will mix in rocks and socks.
Rocks, rocks, rocks!
Socks, socks, socks!

Dad: I will let the pot get hot.
Pop, pop, pop!

Min: The pot is hot, Dad.

Dad: OK. Let's get Zak a big cup of hot mud.

Min: It has jam, gum, rocks,
and socks in it. Yum!

Zak: I do NOT like jam and gum.
I do NOT like rocks and socks.

Min: But you like mud a lot.

Dad: Yes, Zak. Do have a sip.

Min: I bet it will not be bad.

Zak: OK, Dad and Min. Sip!

Dad: Well, do you like it, Zak?

Zak: Sip, sip, BIG sip.

Min: Tell us, Zak. Tell us if you like it!

Zak: Well, I will NOT say "Yuck"…
But I will say a big "YUM!"
Can I get A LOT of it?

Dad: Yes! You can, Zak.

Min: We did it, Dad! We did it!

Dad: Yes, we got Zak to say "Yum."

Zak: Sip, sip, BIG sip. YUM, YUM, YUM!

Hog, Ox, and Mop

3 Characters

High-Frequency Words
be, we, do, go, no, of, to, and, are, for, out, the, good, want, what, with, little

Stretch Word
milk

Hog: I am a big hog.

Ox: I am a big ox.

Mop: I am a big mop.

Hog: Is it odd for a hog and ox
to be pals with a mop?

All: No, no, no!

Ox: It is NOT a bit odd.

Mop: What can we do for fun?

Hog: We can run to the little hut.

Ox: Yes, pals! Let's do it.

All: Run, run, run to the little hut.

Hog: We are at the little hut.

Ox: Do we want to go in the little hut?

Mop: Yes, pals! Let's do it.

All: Run, run, run in the little hut.

Hog: The little hut has a pot of jam.

Ox: The little hut has a bag of buns.

Mop: The little hut has a jug of milk.

All: But we are big. We do not fit!

Hog: BOP! The pot of jam fell.

Ox: BOP! The jug of milk fell.

Mop: BOP! The bag of buns fell.

Hog: Yuck, yuck, yuck!

Ox: What can we do?

Mop: We can fix up the little hut.

Hog: I can lap up the jam.

Ox: I can pick up the buns.

Mop: I can mop up the milk.

All: Lap, lap. Pick, pick. Mop, mop.

Hog: Good job, pals. We did it!

Ox: The little hut is not a mess.

Mop: But the hut is a bit little for us.

Hog: Yes, let's get out of the hut…

Ox: And run in the sun!

Hog: The sun is big.

Mop: The sun is fun.

All: Run, run, run in the sun!

The Big, Big, Big Jet

4 Characters

High-Frequency Words
be, we, do, go, to, all, and, are, see, the, you, have, want, what

Stretch Words
fly, tall, fast

Cab: I am a big cab.

Van: I am a big van.

Bus: I am a big bus.

Jet: I am a big, big, big jet.

Cab: What do you want to do, pals?

Van: Well, we all run on gas.

Bus: And we all can go fast.

Jet: And I have a map to the tall hill.

Cab: I got it! Let's all zip to the tall hill.

Van: OK, pals.

Bus: Get set, zip!

All: Zip, zip, zip to the tall hill.

Cab: We did it! We did it!

Van: Yes, we got to the tall hill.

Bus: But what can we do at the tall hill?

Jet: I got it! The sun will set in a bit.
Let's fly up to the tip top to see it.

Cab: I bet it is fun to see the sun set.
But I am a cab and I can not fly.

Van: And I am a van and I can not fly.

Bus: And I am a bus and I can not fly.

Cab: Sob, sob, sob!

Van: Sob, sob, sob!

Bus: Sob, sob, sob!

Jet: Pals, do not sob and be sad.
I am a jet and I am big, big, big!
If you get in, I will fly you all up
to the tip top of the tall hill.

Cab: Yes, I can fit in Jet.

Van: And I can fit in Jet.

Bus: And I can fit in Jet as well.

Jet: Get in and get set.

Cab: Zip, zip, zip!

Van: Up, up, up!

Bus: Fun, fun, fun!

Jet: We are off to the tip top of the tall hill...

All: to see the sun set!

The Big, Red Hat

1 Reader + 3 Characters

High-Frequency Words
be, we, by, my, so, to, and, the, from, good, have, like, play, that, then, this, went, with, happy

Stretch Word
hello

Reader: Get set! This fun play has kids, a dog, and a big, red hat in it.

Lib: Hello, Bob! I have my big, red hat on.

Bob: Hello, Lib! The hat has dots. I like it a lot.

Lib: I like my hat as well. But I am hot in it.

Bob: Let's run to the fan and sit by it.
Then you will not be hot in the hat.

Lib + Bob: Run, run to the fan!

Reader: But at the fan. . . Lib's hat fell off.
Then it went up, up, up, up!

Lib: My big, red hat! My big, red hat!

Bob: We have to get it back!

Reader: Bob and Lib ran and ran.

Lib + Bob: Get that hat! Get that hat!

Reader: The hat went by a wet duck.
Bob and Lib ran and ran.

Lib + Bob: Get that hat! Get that hat!

Reader: The hat went by a mad cat.
The kids ran and ran.

Lib + Bob: Get that hat! Get that hat!

Reader: The hat went by a tan dog.
Then the dog ran off with it.

Dog: Ruff, ruff, ruff!

Lib: That tan dog has my big, red hat!

Bob: Yes, we have got to get it back.

Reader: Lib and Bob ran and ran.
They got the hat back,
but the dog got sad.

Dog: Sob, sob, sob!

Bob: This is bad. I do not like sad dogs.

Lib: Yes, Bob. But I can fix it.
I will let him have my big, red hat.

Reader: So, the dog got the hat back from Lib.

Bob: This is good. I DO like happy dogs.

Dog: Wag, wag, wag!

Buck Is in the Muck!

5 Characters

High-Frequency Words
be, me, we, of, no, so, to, and, are, the, out, you, help, good, what, with, thank, little

Stretch Word
stuck

Buck: Help me, help me!

Dog: Run, run. What is up, Buck?

Buck: Yuck! I am stuck in the muck.

Dog: Well, I am big and I am fit.
I will tug you out of the muck.

Buck: You are a good pal, Dog.

Dog: Tug, tug, tug!
I had no luck, Buck.

Buck: Yuck! It is not fun to be stuck.

Cub: Run, run. Can I be of help?

Dog: Yes, Cub! Buck is in the muck.
He can not get out.

Cub: I am big and I am fit.
I will tug Buck with you.

Buck: You are good pals, Dog and Cub.

Dog: Tug, tug, tug!

Cub: Tug, tug, tug!

Dog: We had no luck, Buck.

Cub: We can not get you out of the muck.

Buck: Yuck! It is not fun to be stuck.

Yak: Run, run. Can I be of help?

Cub: Yes, Yak! Buck is in the muck.
Dog and I can not get him out.

Yak: I am big and I am fit.
I will tug Buck with you.

Buck: You are good pals,
Dog, Cub, and Yak.

Dog: Tug, tug, tug!

Cub: Tug, tug, tug!

Yak: Tug, tug, tug!

Dog: We had no luck, Buck.

Yak: We can not get you out of the muck.

Buck: Yuck! It is not fun to be stuck.

Duck: Run, run. Can I be of help?

Dog: No, Duck! Buck is in the muck.

Cub: But you are not a bit big,
so you can not help us.

Duck: I am little, but I CAN help.
I CAN, I CAN, I CAN!

Yak: Do not get mad, little Duck.
It is OK. You can tug with us.

Buck: You are good pals, Dog,
Cub, Yak, and Duck.

Dog: Tug, tug, tug!

Cub: Tug, tug, tug!

Yak: Tug, tug, tug!

Duck: Tug, tug, tug!

Buck: POP! You did it! You did it!
I am NOT stuck in the muck!

Dog: No yuck. We had luck.

Buck: Thank you, pals.

Cub: A little duck can…

Yak: be a big help.

Duck: Yes! I CAN, I CAN, I CAN!

Buck: Dog, Cub, Yak, and Duck—
can I get hugs?

All: Hug, hug, hug, hug, hug!